SEVILLE SEASONS

CITY STORIES

Contents

Introduction 5

Spring 9

Early summer 35

Late summer 61

Autumn 87

Winter 113

Contributors 138

Credits 141

Index 142

Introduction

With its thousands of orange trees, rainbow tiles and sea of pastel-toned facades, Seville is a city of colour. The kaleidoscope shimmies and shifts throughout the seasons: the honeyed glint of a sun-warmed tower in spring, the silver-green leaves of an olive branch come autumn, the fluorescent light shows illuminating the stone walls of the old town in December. Sevillanos embrace the changing seasons with an exuberance that matches the theatricality and intensity of the city itself. This reputation for liveliness is expressed on a phenomenally grand scale at its two great festivals – Semana Santa at Easter and, later in April, the Feria de Abril. But it's also embodied in the delicious minutiae of daily life, which is slow, celebratory and centred on food, drink and soaking up the sun. Nothing beats a sip of that first icy beer of the summer on a lively bar terrace or feasting on a paper cone of piping-hot *boquerones en adobo* (marinated and fried anchovies) on an autumnal walk.

Throughout the year, competitions judge flower-filled courtyards tended by devoted dowagers, book fairs pay homage to the city's literary heritage, festivals celebrate everything from cinema to jazz and dance. Then there are the classic annual events: special opera performances hosted in majestic *casa palacios* from March to May, music concerts by moonlight in the Alcázar gardens on sultry summer evenings. Plus, a handful of curious traditions – 'snail season' sees locals slurping down *caracoles* from late April to the end of June, while Noches de La Maestranza transforms the city's bullring into a music stage for one night only in September. Finally, there are the downright fun shenanigans, from flamenco jams, flamingo-spotting and stand-up paddleboarding the Guadalquivir River to the hugely elaborate nativity scenes, or *belenes*, set up in churches across the city at Christmas. Time your visit right, and you'll be swept up in the festivities and frivolities.

Whether you're a first-time visitor or a seasoned Sevillano, this guide is packed with ideas for getting out and about – whatever the month. Visit in spring to catch orange blossom season when the burgeoning clouds of *azahar* perfume the air or embrace Christmas in pleasant climes when the city is alive with festive celebrations. While Seville's temperate weather is precisely what lures travellers to its streets year-round, it is possible to swerve the sizzling summer temperatures in the cool respite of an art gallery, perhaps, or on a breeze-brushed rooftop bar terrace. In this first-ever edition of *Seville Seasons*, our expert travel writers have combed the city for some of the most interesting, offbeat and surprising experiences – at every time of the year.

Spring

*The darkness recedes,
and the souls warm as they cleanse...*

Soak under the stars in a Mudéjar bathhouse

Tucked behind the tangled streets of Santa Cruz, just a stone's throw from the Catedral, AIRE Ancient Baths is one of the city's most compelling wellness escapes. This restored Mudéjar bathhouse, with its string of thermal baths of varying temperatures, is an experience grounded in centuries-old Andalusian tradition, yet unapologetically modern in its execution. Bypass a daytime spa ritual in favour of a late-night experience: it's in the hush of darkness that AIRE comes into its own. Beneath a canopy of stars, the rooftop terrace reveals La Giralda ablaze against the inky sky, a sight that can make even the most jaded spa-goer pause. And that's before a single toe has been dipped into the cornucopia of candlelit pools and saltwater sanctuaries waiting below. Don't miss the red wine bath: designed exclusively for this ancient sanctuary, it beckons bathers to surrender to the antioxidant power of Ribera del Duero's prized Tempranillo grapes – a ritual as indulgent as it is restorative.

🗔 https://beaire.com/en/aire-ancient-baths-sevilla
€ Charge

*...a feast of splendour,
and faithful, joyous days.*

Semana Santa street festivities

Religious processions take place all over Spain during Holy Week, but Seville's is one of the largest and most theatrical. From Palm Sunday to Easter, devout Catholic brotherhoods, called *hermandades*, parade figures of the Virgin Mary and scenes of the crucifixion through the city streets. Burly men carry these elaborate structures – weighing up to 5700kg and laden with flowers and gold – on their backs for up to fourteen hours, while thousands of solemn hooded penitents and explosive marching bands trudge alongside them. Millions of followers flood the city from morning to night, poised at their favourite corner and rushing through the streets to catch a glimpse of the *pasos* (religious floats). The pinnacle of Semana Santa is the dramatic candlelight procession at dawn on Good Friday, when the biggest and most famous parade troops through the night, guided by the light of the moon.

€ Free

*A burst of renewal,
a shock of pink and pomp...*

A flamboyance of flamingos at Dehesa de Abajo

While better known for its beaches and culinary culture, Spain's southern region is among the most important flamingo habitats in Europe. Just an hour's drive from Seville, La Reserva Natural Concertada Dehesa de Abajo is a vast sprawl of soupy marshland, freshwater lagoons and pine forest on the northern edge of the Parque Nacional Coto de Doñana. The wildlife-rich terrain shelters over three hundred bird species, including a colony of pink-plumaged flamingos. Each spring, these leggy waders flock to the shallow marshes, rootling for the best feeding and nesting spots. Wooden pathways wind through the reserve, dotted with strategic observation areas. Venture further south in search of a more elusive resident: the endangered Iberian lynx. Luckily, this spotted beauty is growing in numbers due to the care of the parkkeepers – and a good supply of rabbits.

www.juntadeandalucia.es
Free

*...gives way to frenzied dance,
canopied with grace.*

An insider glimpse of Feria de Abril

The biggest event on Seville's social calendar, the Feria de Abril (Spring Fair) is a week-long extravaganza in April or early May. Beautifully attired men and women – the latter wearing colourful *flamenca* dresses, tight to the hips with frilled skirts, and accessorised to the hilt – feast on plates of garlic-spiked prawns, local cheese and *jamón ibérico*; drink *rebujito* (Manzanilla sherry and lemonade); and dance *sevillanas*, the fun, flirty flamenco-type dance, till the wee hours. The festivities revolve around *casetas* (small tents) – over a thousand fill a vast fairground (*el recinto*) southwest of the city centre, across the bridge from Puerta de Jerez. Most *casetas* are private, making it tricky for visitors. Luckily, there's a large tourist tent where groups can reserve a table for lunch or dinner, soak up the lively atmosphere and try out their moves on the dancefloor.

- https://visitasevilla.es/en/book-your-table-at-the-seville-fair
- € Charge

What sweet scent, from humble petals rise...

Orange blossom season

Seville is home to over 40,000 bitter orange trees, shading cobbled streets, hidden courtyards and leafy parks. For locals, the burgeoning clouds of *azahar* blossoms mark the joyful start of spring. No need to scour the streets for these dainty white blooms, just follow your nose: their sweet aroma perfumes the air and turns heads upwards. The flower only lasts a few weeks, which is why businesses around town like *Heladería Bolas* ice-cream parlour (Calle Herbolarios 20) celebrate with seasonal orange and *azahar* sorbets, available only in the spring. For a treat, book a table at *El Limón* in the *Hotel Don Ramón*, where chef Ali Elkardoudi pays tribute to the local fruit through his *azahar*-laced dessert: *homenaje a la naranja*. The city's emblematic *azahar* oil is sold at the Catedral and specialty shops around town like Tarico (Calle Amor de Dios 14) – the perfect spot to pick up scented soaps, lotions and body oils.

---

www.heladeriasbolas.com; www.hoteldonramon.com
Free, charge for items

...morphing into strident sounds, as senses overwhelmed.

Dance all night at Interestelar Sevilla music festival

Indie music fans mark their diaries every May for Interestelar Sevilla, a two-day festival that welcomes alternative, pop and modern musicians from all around Spain. Hosted in front of a fourteenth-century monastery just outside the Centro Andaluz de Arte Contemporáneo (CAAC), four stages showcase a rotation of artists and DJs, from big names like Fangoria to Rozalén and Amaral. Among the eclectic guitars and flashing lights, some of the most interesting talent perform modern flamenco-esque beats. In addition to cool acts, expect street food, drink stalls, fireworks and artistic exhibitions. The weather can be unpredictable this time of year, so shows don't start until the evening to avoid sizzling temperatures. It's best to buy tickets online in advance, though passes are usually available for last-minute attendees.

- www.interestelarsevilla.com
- € Charge

On the road, the carriages and pilgrims throng...

Pilgrimage to El Rocío

Every year, horsedrawn carriages and processions converge from all over the south of Spain on El Rocío, near Huelva, for the Romería del Rocío, an extraordinary pilgrimage-fair held at the end of May. Whole village communities and local brotherhoods from Huelva, Seville and even Málaga gather in lavishly decorated ox carts and on horseback for the event. As they pass through Seville, you can catch sight of the painted carriages, massive bulls and festive costume. By the time the carts arrive at El Rocío they've been joined by busloads of pilgrims, swelling numbers in recent years to over half a million. Throughout the procession, which climaxes on the Saturday evening, there is dancing and partying. The fair commemorates the miracle of Nuestra Señora del Rocío (Our Lady of the Dew), a statue found in the thirteenth century – so it is said – on this spot and resistant to all attempts to move it elsewhere. The image, credited with all kinds of magic and fertility powers, is paraded before the faithful early on the Sunday morning.

€ Free

*...crafty hands work fast,
and art is formed anew...*

Revel in Seville's artisan scene at Recoveco Market

San Julián, in the northeast of the *casco antiguo* (old town), is a friendly, down-to-earth neighbourhood full of enticing artisan stores. Browse quirky, original fashion, art, ceramics and jewellery – many sustainably and locally produced – and meet Seville's makers. Twice a year, in April or May and December, this creative community holds Recoveco Market, a three-day weekend event in which six stores, workshops and galleries open their doors, showcasing handcrafted wares. Hours vary, but it's usually Friday evening, all day Saturday, and Sunday morning. Look out for Carolina Saiz's illustrated maps; silkscreen-printed fabric bags from The Printed Rabbit; Atelier Potmic's ceramic bowls; Macareno Studio's evocative upcycled art; fine natural toiletries by Fango y Flores; and *The Sevillaner*, a series of artworks emulating New Yorker covers themed around Sevillano tropes.

- https://recovecomarket.com
- Free entry

*...as artisans of old,
leave a trace for new makers.*

Follow the cultural trail to Santa Cruz

The beauty of Santa Cruz, with its tangle of narrow alleys, pastel-hued facades and clouds of colourful flora, has stirred the imagination of many an artist. The medieval Jewish quarter's most famous *barrio* residents were Murillo and Valdés Leal, who painted the Baroque frescoes adorning the Hospital de los Venerables. Today, the district retains its crackling creative energy. Established galleries like longstanding stalwart Rafael Ortiz (Calle Mármoles 12), housed in an eighteenth-century palace, and Galería Haurie (Calle Guzmán el Bueno 9) have paved the way for a string of emerging art hubs. Among these are Espacio Derivado (Plaza Cristo de Burgos 17), a cultural centre hosting talks, exhibitions, film screenings, live music and other events, and Espacio Sacáis (Plaza de la Alianza 3), a gallery providing a platform for young artists from Andalucía.

---

www.galeriarafaelortiz.com; www.galeriahaurie.com; www.espacioderivado.com

€ Free entry

A luminescence descends on the mountainside...

A road trip through the White Towns

Andalucía is dotted with small, brilliantly whitewashed settlements – the Pueblos Blancos or "White Towns". Arguably the finest lie in a roughly triangular area between Seville, Algeciras and Málaga; at its centre is the spectacular town of Ronda. Built on an isolated mountain ridge, it's split in half by a gaping river gorge, spanned by an eighteenth-century arched bridge. From Ronda, almost any car journey to the north or west is rewarding, taking you past a string of White Towns, many fortified since the days of the Reconquest from the Moors. The best of all the routes is to Cádiz via Grazalema, Ubrique and Medina Sidonia. This passes through the spectacular Parque Natural de la Sierra de Grazalema before skirting the nature reserve of Cortes de la Frontera and, towards Alcalá de los Gazules, running through the northern fringe of Parque Natural de los Alcornocales, which derives its name from the forests of cork oaks – the largest of its kind in Europe.

€ Free

*...devoted dowagers,
patios bloom under their gaze...*

Festival of the Patios in Córdoba

Hooked around a loop of the Guadalquivir upstream from Seville, Córdoba might be most famous for its magnificent Moorish mosque, La Mezquita, but it is just as renowned for its tremendous and often wildly extravagant courtyards. The city pushes this architectural form with Fiesta de los Patios, recognised by UNESCO as an Intangible Cultural Heritage of Humanity. Held every May, the twelve-day event is well worth coinciding with a day-trip from Seville, under an hour by train. The most characteristic district for these courtyards is the Alcázar Viejo, between the Alcázar and the parish of San Basilio, though you will discover an abundance in Santa Marina, around the Iglesia de San Lorenzo and near La Magdalena. There is also a scattering of beautiful old courtyards in the old Jewish quarter around La Mezquita. However, one of the standouts is to be found at the Palacio del Marqués de Viana, home to a string of twelve flower-filled patios.

€ Free

*...the walls tell a tale,
of ignoble, quixotic history.*

A literary tour in Cervantes' footsteps

In 1916, 25 ceramic plaques were put up around Seville, plastered on buildings linked to the Golden Age writer, Cervantes. Today, nineteen remain, each displaying the epithet 'The Prince of Spanish Wits' and a portrait of the man himself, and it is possible to follow in the footsteps of the great author by tracing this so-called Ruta de los Azulejos, or Tile Route. Many of the locations are associated with his most iconic work, *Don Quixote*, which he wrote partly in Seville, while others mark connections with his Exemplary Novels, particularly *Rinconete y Cortadillo*, a bleak portrayal of the city's seventeenth-century underbelly. The route through the *casco antiguo* captures Seville's moment as Europe's 'Great Babylon', from the steps of the Catedral by the Puerta del Perdón, where the eponymous pickpockets sought their prey, to Plaza de San Francisco, or the colourful houses of Calle Betis, home to their criminal enterprise.

€ Free

Early summer

*The brightest days,
tolerant and open...*

Dance, drinks and drag at Seville's Pride

Spain was the third country in the world to legalise same-sex marriage, and its Pride festivals are some of the biggest and brightest. El Orgullo festivities run all through the month of June in Seville – art expositions, historical neighbourhood tours, theatre productions – and culminate with three days of music, dance and drag in the long tree-lined plaza of the Alameda. Thursday's *pregón* (opening speech), usually given by a famous Spanish personality, kicks off the celebrations and is followed by a stream of outdoor concerts and *discotecas* pumping out dance-ready hits. Saturday's colourful parade marks the finale, with jubilant crowds marching from the Plaza Don Juan de Austria, passing through downtown, and ending in the Alameda, where revellers keep the party going into the small hours of the morning.

www.sevilla.org/actualidad/archivos-pdf/programa-orgullo-1.pdf

Free

*...beckon you on high,
the hubbub below removed.*

Rooftop drinks with a view

In the hotter months, when the mercury creeps above 30°C, cool respite beckons above the streets at a rooftop bar. Most high-end hotels feature lofty breeze-tousled terraces with views of the Catedral and La Giralda, as well as other iconic monuments dotting the city's skyline such as the towers of Plaza de España, the undulating curves of Las Setas or the César Pelli-designed Torre Sevilla, the tallest building in Andalucía. Some of the best rooftop spots in town include *Level 5th* at *Ribera de Triana*, overlooking the river; *La Terraza del EME* atop the *Hotel EME Catedral Mercer*, with views into the neighbouring basílica's Patio de los Naranjos; *La Terraza del Hotel Inglaterra*, with a tree-filled vista of Plaza Nueva; *La Terraza Doña Maria*, from where La Giralda glows pinky-orange at sunset; and chic *Scalpers Rooftop* at the *Radisson Magdalena Plaza*. Visit over the weekend to sip on cocktails to a soundtrack of live DJs or musicians.

- Various
- Free entry

Contemporary and classical collide, actors weaving magic by night...

Party with locals at Icónica Santalucía Sevilla Fest

Few concerts boast a venue as splendid as Icónica Santalucía's: Plaza de España, a huge semicircular complex decorated with locally made ceramic tiles and bubbling fountains, illuminated in colour by night. In June and July, this stunning setting provides a backdrop for performances by the best Spanish and international artists. Past stars at the music festival have included Pet Shop Boys, Justin Timberlake and Kylie Minogue. The unique, characterful space is intimate and historic rather than large and soulless, accommodating up to 18,000 concertgoers, though numbers usually hover around 12,000. In addition to live music, the weeks-long event features DJ sets, bars and food vans dishing up the likes of bull's tails croquettes, fried calamari and pork *montaditos* (grilled sandwiches). To beat the sultry heat, acts usually kick off after dark, around 10.30pm.

- https://iconicafest.com
- Charge

...serenading in regal rooms, casts harmonious spells.

Watch opera in a palace

Birthplace of *Carmen*, *Don Giovanni* and the *Barber of Seville*, the City of Opera has stirred the imagination of many a composer. From March to May, three *casa palacios* (large mansions) put on adapted versions of these operatic masterpieces performed by a pared-down cast of costumed singers – around three to five – with piano accompaniment. The majestic spaces become their stage: *Carmen* at Palacio de Las Dueñas, home to Spanish grandee the nineteenth-century Duque de Alba; *Don Giovanni* at Las Salinas' magnificent stucco arches; and the *Barber of Seville* at the Baroque salmon-pink Hospital de la Caridad. When the exquisite arias of Bizet, Mozart and Rossini fill the beautiful, arcaded patios of private palaces and grand edifices, it makes for a memorable evening. Duration is about 75 minutes; arrive early to bag a good seat.

€ Charge

*Slow the pace,
and savour the heat...*

Slurp down caracoles in snail season

Come late April, you'll spot blackboards spring up across the city, scrawled in chalk with the words *Hay caracoles* ('There are snails'). Helpfully, they are often accompanied by a cheerful illustration of the creatures in question. Meanwhile, great tubs of the crawling critters are sold on street corners, and plates of discarded shells tower atop bar tables. Seville's eagerly awaited snail season has arrived. When it comes to this spring delicacy, there are two main options: dainty *caracoles* in a salty, heavily flavoured *caldo* (broth), or larger *cabrillas*, typically served in a rich, tomato-based sauce. Both are best washed down with a cold Cruzcampo. The season finishes at the end of June, mind, so be quick – snails need not apply. Good places to sample the speciality are *El Cerezo* (Avenida Dr. Fedriani) in Macarena; *Bodega Umbrete* (Plaza Pumarejo 89) or *Casa Vizcaíno* (Calle Feria 27) in the *casco antiguo*; or *Casa Ruperto* (Avenida Santa Cecilia 2) in Triana.

https://casavizcaino.es
Charge

*...then quicken your step,
a swish of a skirt, a blur of feet...*

Flamenco jams at Ánima Galería Taberna

Seville is part of the Flamenco Triangle, one of three places in Andalucía where the art form supposedly originates, so where better to watch a soul-stirring performance? However, it's best to avoid the touristy *tablaos* offering fixed shows – most of which are tacky and expensive. For a more authentic and spontaneous experience, *Ánima Galería Taberna* is the answer. This ancient, ample, no-frills wine bar in the San Lorenzo district hosts twice-weekly flamenco jams. Guests don't pay to enter, and the dancers and musicians play purely for the pleasure of each other's company. This is a serious venue, so it's important to be respectful, but on a given night you're apt to experience amazing virtuoso displays from local guitarists and singers and performances by students from the nearby academy. The loose, convivial energy will linger in your bones long after you've left.

---

https://animataberna.wordpress.com
€ Free

*...away from urban energy,
tranquillity and grandeur meet.*

Palatial opulence at Casa de Pilatos

The Santa Cruz neighbourhood is studded with fine aristocratic mansions, but by far the finest is the Casa de Pilatos, built by the Marqués de Tarifa on his return from a pilgrimage to Jerusalem in 1519 and popularly thought to have been in imitation of the house of Pontius Pilate. In fact, it's an interesting and harmonious mixture of Mudéjar, Gothic and Renaissance styles, featuring dazzling *azulejos*, a tremendous sixteenth-century stairway and one of the most elegant domestic patios in the city. The finest tilework adorns the staircase, which is crowned by a gold-hued *artesonado* dome; the first floor is available to visit by guided tour. Look out for the century-spanning portraits of the ducal Medinaceli family, some of whom still partly occupy the mansion.

https://fundacionmedinaceli.org
€ Charge

Society divided: no smoke without fire, Bizet's heroine is brought to life.

Step inside the real-life set of Carmen

Immediately south of the Alcázar, the fortress-like Antigua Fábrica de Tabacos is the setting for Bizet's masterpiece, *Carmen*. The old tobacco factory was built in the 1750s and, in its heyday, contributed to Seville's phenomenal wealth from a monopoly on trade with America. At its peak in the 1800s, it was the country's largest single employer. The factory packed in a workforce of some four thousand women, *cigarreras*, who made the cigars and cigarettes by hand. Many were Roma from Triana – the inspiration for Bizet's fiery tragic heroine. The French composer's opera, primarily set in Seville during the early nineteenth century, revolves around the passionate and free-spirited factory worker Carmen and her turbulent relationships, particularly with the soldier Don José and the bullfighter Escamillo. The factory is now part of the University of Seville, with free tours on weekday mornings (book in advance).

- visitasevilla.es/en/tobacco-factory
- Free tours

*Beneath the earth,
our past is scored in stone...*

Go underground at Cueva de la Pileta

Under a two-hour drive southeast of Seville, Cueva de la Pileta is a subterranean complex of caverns scored with remarkable prehistoric cave paintings of animals (mainly bison), fish and magic symbols. These etchings date occupation of the cave back as far as 25,000 BC – predating the more famous caves at Altamira in northern Spain – through to the end of the Bronze Age. It's well worth a day-trip from Seville, especially if combined with a visit to the extraordinary mountaintop city of Ronda. You can only visit the caves by daily guided tours (booking essential), which last an hour on average, but can be longer, and are in Spanish – though guides can speak a little English. Hundreds of bats flitter around the gloomy corners of the cave, illuminated only by the lanterns carried by visitors (there's no artificial lighting).

https://cuevadelapileta.es
€ Charge

*...the ribbon of gold,
a rich resting place.*

Sunset riverside picnics by the Guadalquivir

Once you've ticked off all the big-hitting sights, eaten your body weight in tapas and covered every inch of the city's cobbled streets on foot, why not do as the locals do and picnic by the river? Early summer, when the nights are long and the city is drenched in golden light, is an ideal time to soak in a slower-paced Seville. Pick up some chilled Cruzcampo and regional snacks – try *jamón ibérico de Jabugo*, payoyo cheese from Cádiz and Jaén olives – then head down to the pistachio-coloured Guadalquivir River. Next to the Puente de Isabel II, you'll find the best spot in town: a sandy flagstone suntrap overlooking the pastel-hued houses of Calle Betis. Unroll your blanket, lay out the feast and watch as locals zip along the river in rowing boats while tourists march across the famous bridge above. While away the evening people-watching until the sun casts its final honeyed rays over Triana on the other side of the water.

 Free

*Further riches of varying vintage,
are waiting to be found...*

Hunt for treasure at Mercadillo del Jueves

Every Thursday from 9am, colourful stalls spring up along Calle Feria as the city's biggest flea market, or *mercadillo* (also known as Jueves Market), comes to life. The offering is eclectic – the vendors even more so. Rummage through stacks of vintage art, antiques, old books, crockery, flamenco dresses, the odd Singer sewing machine or birdcage, and much more. It's a great place to stroll even if you don't buy anything; the vibe is lively, and you'll rub shoulders with locals browsing through the heaps of time-worn treasures. You can pick up gourmand treats at the eighteenth-century Mercado de Feria – the oldest food market in Seville – up by the Parroquia de Omnium Sanctorum. Though the opening hours are notoriously unreliable, you'll usually find at least a few tapas bars open and a smattering of food stalls.

 Free

*...seaward-bound vessels,
weaving needlework along the golden river.*

Join the Virgen del Carmen procession

Revered in maritime cities around Spain and beyond, the Virgen del Carmen is the patron saint of sailors and fishermen, protecting all those at sea. Every year on and around 16 July, statues of the Virgin are paraded through the streets, accompanied by live bands and the adoring local community, and thence to the sea in boats. While Seville is not a coastal port, the Guadalquivir River played a key part in the city's history. Two images of the Virgin are taken along the river on separate days, escorted by smaller vessels in a spectacular fluvial procession: the Carmen de Calatrava emerges from her simple chapel in the Alameda and sails from the Puente de la Barqueta, while the Carmen del Puente departs from Paseo Nuestra Señora de la O next to Triana Bridge. Watching these effigies glide along the water is a surreal and mesmerising experience.

€ Free

Late summer

*Staging of a different era,
dance as shimmering day escapes...*

Festival fever at a Roman theatre

Just outside Seville lie the remains of the first Roman city in the Iberian Peninsula: Itálica, a great sprawl of crumbling temples, mosaics and thermal baths. *Game of Thrones* fans will likely recognise the immaculately preserved theatre as the backdrop of the Well of Dragons from the seventh season. Today, the amphitheatre pulsates with energy once again when the International Dance Festival of Itálica comes to town in June. Artists from around the globe take to the stage with late-night performances showcasing modern dance ensembles; a number of Spanish acts boast a contemporary flamenco flair. Itálica is easily accessed via bus, taxi or rideshare from Seville, making a night out at this underrated archaeological site a must.

- www.festivalitalica.es
- € Charge

...pulsing night, where moon and music beat down, upon the flora and fauna.

Music by moonlight in the Alcázar gardens

Every summer, from late June to mid-September, jazz beats, oud strums and flute trills waft through the gardens of the Alcázar. The Noches en los Jardines del Real Alcázar concert season sees evening performances next to the Pabellón de Carlos V, a tiled pavilion that starred in the *Game of Thrones*. The backdrop to the stage: the storybook sixteenth-century Galería de los Grutesco lined with Mudéjar arches. In this magical setting, hear groups play genres from flamenco, blues and swing, to classical, antique, European and world music. One of the most unusual is Sephardic music, originating from the medieval (pre-Inquisition) Jewish population of Spain and Portugal – Seville had the largest community after Toledo. The events start at 10.30pm, but concertgoers can wander around the serene grounds, beneath palms swaying in the night breeze, from 9pm.

https://alcazarsevilla.org
€ Charge

*The art of movement,
a seam from past to present…*

Learn flamenco with the best guide in town

A flamenco show is a must on a trip to Seville. But to dive deeper, head across Puente de Isabel II to Triana – arguably one of the birthplaces of the emblematic *andaluz* art form – for a class with Eva Izquierdo to appreciate what it takes to master this complex Spanish dance. An hour in the studio is also a great workout and a cool air-conditioned escape from the oppressive summer heat. Eva's enlightening sessions are all about having a good time and helping visitors grasp the nuances of this important aspect of local culture. You can even rent a traditional getup (skirt, shawl and shoes) to really get in the mood. After having taken a class yourself, the experience of watching a flamenco performance in one of the many Triana *tablaos* takes on deeper levels of meaning and understanding.

- www.ishowusevilla.com
- Charge

...bearing down the golden thread, with slow, deliberate strokes.

Paddle the Guadalquivir

The Guadalquivir, one of the only navigable rivers in Spain, is an important piece of Seville's cultural jigsaw. The waterway was the starting point of the first round-the-world voyage, led by Ferdinand Magellan in 1519 and continued by Juan Sebastián Elcano. On a sizzling summer's day, the best way to explore the city is by stand-up paddleboard or kayak. Guided tours begin at the Torre del Oro, an old Moorish defence tower once plastered in honeyed tiles that still glows gold (*oro*) at sunset, and wend past the Espacio Exploraterra and the life-size replica *Nao Victoria 500*, the ship that sailed the first worldwide expedition. Further upriver looms the Plaza de Toros de la Real Maestranza, one of the most significant bullrings in Spain and dating back to 1761. Glide beneath the Puente de Isabel II, a nineteenth-century bridge that leaps across the water to Triana, before returning downriver to catch a final glimpse of the famed towers of Plaza de España in the distance.

- https://supguadalquivir.com
- € Charge

*Cleansing stirs the senses,
as a taste of history warms in shade...*

Tapas in an ancient Arabic bathhouse

Looking out over La Giralda, *Cervecería Giralda* has long been a favourite bar with both locals and visitors since it opened in 1923. But in 2021, during extensive renovations, workers discovered a secret hiding beneath the floor: an almost intact twelfth-century Islamic bathhouse. Built at the time of the Almohad Caliphate, it would have once been one of the most luxurious hammams in Seville, with a prime location right next to the Alcázar and the Great Aljama Mosque. Today, it's an atmospheric setting in which to sip glasses of wine and nibble on plates of tapas – sitting beneath domes decorated with star-shaped skylights and painted in original frescoes in one of the best-preserved bathhouses in all of Spain. It's also a cool underground respite from the intense summer heat. Enjoy classic plates such as oxtail stew, pork cheeks and cured meats or more modern offerings like shitake mushrooms stuffed with *pico de gallo* (salsa).

> https://cerveceriagiralda.es
> € Charge

*...honeyed sun upon a nectar breathes,
but tempered by an icy grasp.*

Beat the heat with an icy beer

Sevillanos take their cold beer seriously, especially when the temperatures tip over 40ºC. Locally made Cruzcampo, a light pilsner, is the tipple of choice and is usually served in half-pint glasses (*cañas*) or small bottles – *botellines* – to prevent it from losing its chill. Few places serve it as cool as *La Federal* on Calle Feria. Bottles at this barebones bar teeter on the brink of freezing, with a chunk of ice attached and a metal plate to catch the water as it melts. Just a few steps down the street, *Casa Vizcaíno* is a neighbourhood institution famous for pouring icy *cañas* from the tap. *El Tremendo* by the Plaza Ponce de León is another classic haunt or check out *Moraleja* on Calle Zaragoza for ultra-refreshing sips and a succinct list of seasonal tapas like *salmorejo de melón*, a fruity twist on cold soup native to southern Spain.

---

https://linktr.ee/moralejasevilla;
www.instagram.com/lafederalbarsevilla;
www.instagram.com/casavizcainosevilla

€ Charge

*A perimeter of yesteryear,
charts a story of royal passage.*

Walk the walls of La Muralla Almohade

Next to the Arco de la Macarena lies the largest chunk of the ancient Moorish city walls – La Muralla Almohade – dating back to 1105. While you may spot smaller portions of the pink-tinted fortifications around town, this is by far the most impressive, punctuated with eight towers, narrow entryways and battlement-studded walkways. The city is currently restoring the structure and in time visitors will be able to climb the tower and walk along parts of the wall. Stroll below the ramparts, either inside the city or outside along the grassy knoll, as you gaze over the tenth-century butter-yellow fortress beneath you. Be sure to allow some time for the Arco de la Macarena, one of only three remaining city gates in the original walls, which served as the royal entryway for the kings and queens of the period.

 Free

*Mediterranean influences offer
sweet relief in sultry months...*

A slice of Italy in Seville at a gelato parlour

Ice cream is essential in Seville during the sweltering summer months, and the best can be found in an Italian-style gelato shop just off Alameda de Hércules: *Freskura*. It's a local favourite – and it's easy to see why. Seasonal fruit flavours like fig showcase local ingredients in one tantalising swirl of deliciousness. For an uber-reviving option, grapefruit *granita* (shaved ice) takes the edge off the blistering midday sun. If classic Italian specialities are more your jam, you're in luck: traditional options like pistachio, *nocciola* (hazelnut) and rich chocolate consistently hit the mark. Plus, if you're vegan or have a dairy intolerance, you can still revel in the gourmand treat thanks to a selection of plant-based options. Take a peek into the kitchen from the street (Calle Vulcano 4) to watch the team work their gelato magic.

 Charge

*...salty spirits are awoken,
in the theatre of athletic might.*

Catch a football game with die-hard fans

Sevillanos are football-mad, and loyalties run deep. The city is divided between the more conservative, traditional Sevilla FC supporters and the working-class fanatics of Real Betis Balompié – Baetis was the Roman name for the Guadalquivir River. While most international fans flock to the Ramón Sánchez-Pizjuán Stadium to see Sevilla in late summer, those in the know bag home tickets to see Betis, or Los Verdiblancos (the green and whites), at Estadio Benito Villamarín. It was once true that Sevilla was the better team, having won the Europa League seven times, but Betis have been creeping higher in the table than its red-shirted rivals in recent years. Expect scarf-wielding fans streaming from bars and sunflower seeds (*pipas*) crunching underfoot on the terraces. Goosebumps are almost guaranteed when the team sprints out to the club's operatic anthem. If you want to fit in, join chants of "Viva el Betis manque pierda', meaning "Long live Betis even if they lose".

---

www.realbetisbalompie.es
€ Charge

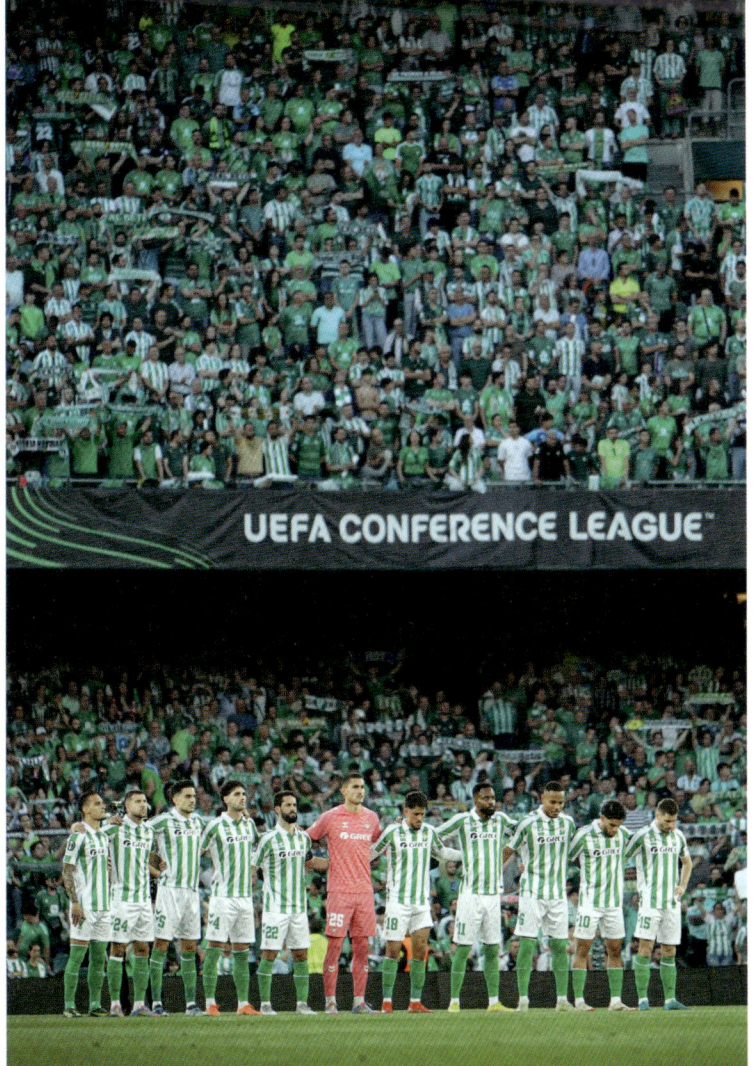

*Sizzling scales sear in season,
and are savoured...*

Feast on fried fish like a local

Andalucía is known in Spain as the *zona de los fritos* (fried food zone). Plates of crispy *chanquetes* (whitebait), sardines, *calamares* and *boquerones* (anchovies) are all *andaluz* favourites. Dating back to 1928, *Freiduría Puerta de la Carne* in Seville's *casco antiguo* (old town) serves some of the freshest *pescaítos fritos* (fried fish) at wallet-friendly prices. The city's oldest – and most famous – fry shop may look unassuming from the outside, but its sea-tinged delicacies are legendary in these parts. This casual eatery is a great pit stop for a leisurely, sun-soaked lunch on the outdoor dining terrace. A paper cone overflowing with piping-hot *boquerones en adobo* (marinated and fried anchovies) is worth any wait you may encounter.

www.freiduriapuertadelacarne.com/freiduria-sevilla
€ Charge

*...piety on a humbler scale,
tradition and festivity intertwine.*

Feria de Santa Ana in Triana

A smaller, more local and much older version of the main Seville *feria*, the Velá de Santa Ana brings the streets of Triana to life in the third week of July. The *velá* is named for the Virgin Mary's mother, to whom the city's oldest parish church, located nearby, is dedicated. Public *casetas* (tents) line the riverfront side of Calle Betis from the Puente de Isabel II. Skewered sardines, *espetos*, are grilled over hot coals, while beer and *tinto con blanca* (red wine with soda) flow freely. Don't miss the *cucaña* – young men try to walk across a greasy pole extending from a boat over the river, aiming to snatch a flag at the end to win a cash prize. It's an entertaining spectacle as they wobble precariously and then (usually) splash into the water. From around 10pm, live bands perform on a stage in Plaza de Altozano, and the party continues late into the night. Fireworks at midnight on the last day mark the *velá*'s close.

€ Free

*Art pauses time and passes time,
within a moment.*

A dose of culture at CaixaForum

Next to the Torre Sevilla, just over the river from Plaza de Armas, CaixaForum hosts world-class exhibitions developed in collaboration with the likes of the Prado, British Museum or Louvre, but without the high prices or crowds. Recent shows have explored themes like art and nature, featuring iconic artists such as Picasso, Georgia O'Keefe and Giacometti; children can enjoy related educational yet fun activities. In addition to the blissfully air-conditioned galleries, there is an excellent gift shop stocking Seville-themed books and artistic pieces, plus a café with a spacious terrace and occasional live music. Immersive audio-visual experiences, concerts, creative workshops for all ages, and themed weeks dedicated to art, music, science and cinema complete the offering. Selected events, like percussion workshops and tap-dancing classes, are free to attend.

https://caixaforum.org
€ Charge

Autumn

Learned masters change to childish tales in the pages, turning, as the seasons refresh anew...

Bookish days at Feria del Libro Sevilla

From Moorish philosophers to twentieth-century poets and today's modern creatives, Seville has inspired writers throughout the centuries to wax lyrical about its colourful flora and tranquil patios. In October, the city celebrates its literary heritage with the Feria del Libro Sevilla, an outdoor book fair held in the Jardines de Murillo. Named after the city's famous painter who was born next door, the public park previously pertained to the Alcázar's palace gardens but was gifted to the city in 1911. Over fifty stalls are helmed by bookshops and publishing houses from around Spain, while tents host author readings and book signings. Though most titles, including comics, children's stories, cookbooks and magazines, are in Spanish, a handful of stands sell English-language editions. Be sure to browse the collections of vintage classics to scope out one-off finds like *Don Quixote*.

---

https://ferialibrosevilla.com
€ Free

*...rolling and flickering on and on,
scenes across the smoothest screen.*

A film festival for cinephiles

Every November, Seville hosts the prestigious Festival de Cine Europeo, or European Film Festival, with screenings and events held in a handful of theatres around the city. The nine-day shindig brings together some of the most talented filmmakers on the continent, many of whom host interesting Q&A sessions after their cinematic previews. While practically all popular films in Spain are dubbed, festival movies are shown in their original language with Spanish subtitles. Most showings cost less than €4, and discounted bonus packs are available for those looking to dive headfirst into independent European cinema. Events sell out quickly so be sure to purchase tickets in advance online.

https://festivalcinesevilla.eu
€ Charge

As its ramparts, the city's ambrosia fortified, fiery and fragrant, no bitter regret to taste...

Sip Seville's golden elixir

When the fierce summer heat begins to ease, there's no better way to toast the arrival of autumn than with a glass of *vino de naranja*. This amber-hued fortified wine, gently infused with the peels of Seville's famed bitter oranges, has been savoured here for centuries, a taste as evocative as the *azahar*-scented breeze drifting through the city's narrow streets. Served chilled, sometimes over ice, this golden elixir offers notes of candied orange, honey and a whisper of spice. Skip the tourist spots and head instead to *Taberna Álvaro Peregil* (Calle Mateos Gago 22), commonly known as *La Goleta* ('The Schooner'), a timeworn *bodeguita* just steps from the Catedral, owned by Álvaro Peregil, son of the renowned late flamenco singer Pepe Peregil. So tiny you might just blink and miss it, *La Goleta* is one of the few places still offering the original eighteenth-century recipe. The perfect aperitif before a slow Andalusian supper, it delivers a lesser-known but time-honoured taste of Seville's enduring love affair with its celebrated fruit.

 Charge

...coming to life at dusk, not bound by sleep, twilight warmed by laughter and play.

Visit museums and galleries after dark

Balmy autumn evenings in Seville see squares and avenues buzzing with people, often to a soundtrack of live music. However, for one night in October, galleries and museums open their doors to the public for free to kick off the city's cultural season. On the first Friday of the month, Noche en Blanco is marked with a whole host of activities, from guided art routes to microplays, pottery workshops to dance performances, concerts to church visits. With more than 125 events at various venues like Baroque gem Iglesia de San Luis de los Franceses, futuristic Pabellón de Navegación and the CaixaForum, it's easy to fill the evening hopping between fascinating places, some of which are usually closed to the public.

€ Free

Rebellion ripens in modest surroundings, dissenting voices strong and true...

Culture and community in La Fuga Librerías

If you're looking for the beating heart of leftist intellectual culture in Seville, then venture no further than a tiny bookshop discretely tucked next to the Alameda de Hércules, a restored plaza converted from one of the oldest public parks in Europe (established by the Visigoths when they rerouted the Guadalquivir). La Fuga Librerías, helmed by a rangy old anarchist with an almost uniform contempt for his customers, routinely holds lectures on everything from Spanish Marxism to contemporary poetry. On a given night, you're apt to hear an impassioned chronicle of Andalusian feminism, a diatribe against regional exploitation by big agricultural concerns, a Dadaist poetry reading, or a chat about new forms in Spanish fiction. This isn't the most tourist-friendly spot – don't expect anyone to go out of their way to speak English to you – but if you love literature and are curious about Andalusian politics and culture, you could do a lot worse than to explore the shelves – and minds – of La Fuga.

https://lafugalibrerias.com
Free

...raging bulls make way for ringing notes by moonlight in this sonorous circle.

Catch a concert at Noches de La Maestranza

Every autumn, Seville's historic bullring hosts not fights, but concerts, in a celebration of beauty, sound and culture. In early September, the Noches de La Maestranza brings together some of the most renowned Spanish and global musicians in a moonlit gig beneath star-studded skies. The Plaza de Toros de la Real Maestranza is one of the most iconic monuments in the city, painted in meringue-white and lemon-yellow, with elegant arches and a grand facade. Built in 1761, it is one of the most important bullrings in Spain, both from an architectural and cultural perspective. Typically, the way to explore it and see inside would be to book a ticket to watch a bullfight or visit the museum. However, this magical festival offers visitors the chance to experience a piece of Seville history and design without having to support the controversial ancient spectacle.

- https://nochesdelamaestranza.com
- € Charge

Mountainous reaches sink to cavernous expanse, echoing with the rosy past.

Subterranean treasures at Gruta de las Maravillas

Just over an hour's drive northwest of Seville, Aracena is the highest town in the Sierra Morena – the longest of Spain's mountain ranges. Aracena's principal attraction, along with its award-winning *jamón ibérico*, is Gruta de las Maravillas, the largest and arguably most impressive cave in the country. Supposedly discovered by a local boy in search of a lost pig, the cavern is now illuminated and there are guided tours as soon as a couple of dozen or so people have gathered. On Sunday, there's a constant procession, but usually plenty of time to gaze and wonder. The cave is astonishingly beautiful, and amusing to visit, too – the last chamber of the tour is known as the Sala de los Culos (Room of the Buttocks), its walls and ceiling an outrageous, naturally sculpted exhibition, tinged in a pinkish-orange light.

www.aracena.es

€ Charge

The pince-nez of the streets will help you see, taking it all in with clarity...

Explore the city on two wheels

Autumn is perhaps the best time to explore Seville on two wheels, when temperatures start to dip and crowds wane. Few realise Seville is one of Spain's most bike-friendly cities, with over 180km of green-painted cycling lanes and a decent bike-sharing scheme. Sign up for a guided tour or strike out solo to trace the contours of the Guadalquivir, skirt the grand Alcázar and cruise through Parque de María Luisa, pausing for breath outside Plaza de España, an impressive display of traditional Sevillano architecture. Film fans may recognise the twentieth-century square from *Star Wars: Attack of the Clones* or *Lawrence of Arabia*. More serious cyclists may wish to download Komoot, a bike-mapping app that's packed with routes snaking in and around Seville and out to the Andalusian countryside.

---

www.biketourseville.com
€ Charge

...a backstreet scape for urbane denizens, framed by statuesque architecture.

Art in Alfalfa

Alfalfa may be a tourist enclave, but you only have to duck down the narrow sidestreets shooting off the main plaza to stumble across an unexpected cultural scene. The area around the square, occasionally referred to as the Soho of Seville, is peppered with hidden art galleries and cool creative spaces. At Calle Don Alonso el Sabio 8, the studio and gallery of contemporary artist Jaime Abaurre can be found in Más Cara Que Espalda, a building designed by the architect behind the Plaza de España. Here, Abaurre showcases his minimalist Pop Art drawings, from black-and-white line illustrations to colourful post-Impressionist designs. Down the street, Delimbo, at Calle Pérez Galdós 1, features rotating collections of modern art, including paintings, sculptures and large-scale installations. The intimate Berlín Galería (Calle Boteros 4) is the brainchild of Jesús Barrera and highlights both emerging and established artists; exhibitions rotate every six weeks – if you happen to stumble upon an opening night, the party will be in full swing.

- https://mascaraqueespalda.com; www.delimbo.com; www.barrerabaldan.com
- Free

*Pricked with vampiric flame,
carmine spirits illuminate the dungeon dark...*

Gothic grandeur at Bar Garlochí

Garlochí deserves its unofficial accolade as the oddest drinking den in Seville – no mean feat in a city with more bars than hospital beds. It would be easy to think the design of the place is a put-on, or steeped in irony, but the owners are deadly serious. *Bar Garlochí* could be modelled on a church or funeral home. The floor is plush, blood-red carpeting, the walls plastered with devotional photos of the Virgin or the Passion of the Christ, the smell of incense is intoxicating, and every table is cumbered with enormous, mottled wax candles that look like they've been burning for a thousand years. Until recently the owners refused to serve liquor (that way lies sin, after all) but relented and it is now a great spot for grabbing a crisp Cruzcampo or, if you're feeling adventurous, its signature Sangre de Cristo, or 'Blood of Christ', a punchy grenadine and cava mix. If you want to skip the Semana Santa crowds but still feel like you're in the middle of the Procession of the Good Death, *Garlochí* (Calle Boteros 26) is your spot.

€ Charge for drinks

*...what bounty flows from sun-kissed hills,
gold and green mix in graded groves.*

Autumnal specialities for foodies

Given that Andalucía is Spain's largest producer of olive oil, especially known for its extra-virgin varieties, Seville-bound foodies will want to savour the region's renowned 'liquid gold'. Autumn is arguably the best season to visit local olive farms. At this time of year, Seville's outlying, undulating grove-dappled hills are especially magical: the silvery grey-green leaves of gnarled olive trees bathed in golden sunlight. Glowing scenery aside, harvesting typically takes place from October, which heralds opportunities to witness, or even participate in, age-old processing traditions, alongside touring groves and sampling new-harvest oils. Such is the case at *Hacienda Merrha*. Located in the Los Alcores countryside, to the east of Seville, this family-run farm produces several esteemed varieties of extra-virgin Basilippo olive oil, and its cultural centre and tasting tours offer immersive insights into local specialties in aromatic surroundings.

https://basilippo.com/en/experiences
€ Charge

*A mausoleum but no haunting chills,
preserving beauty in an ancient cemetery.*

Unearth Roman ruins at Carmona

An easy day-trip from Seville, Carmona might be a small, sleepy town today, but it was once an important Roman city – with an extraordinary subterranean necropolis to prove it. The ancient burial site, set across a low cypress-studded hill, shelters over nine hundred family tombs dating from the second century BC to the fourth century AD. Enclosed in underground rock-hewn chambers, the tombs are often frescoed and contain niches lined with still-intact funeral urns. Some have vestibules with stone benches for funeral banquets, and several retain carved family emblems (one is of an elephant, perhaps symbolic of long life). Most spectacular is the Tumba de Servilia – a huge colonnaded temple with vaulted side chambers. Before you leave Carmona, check out the Puerta de Córdoba, an imposing Roman gateway to the ancient Córdoba road – once the mighty Via Augusta heading north to Zaragoza, Gaul and finally Rome itself.

€ Charge

Winter

Colour kaleidoscopes like snowflakes across a chilling land, mesmerising amid winter's creep…

A festive light and music extravaganza

At Christmas time, the scent of roasting chestnuts fills the air as colourful lights brighten around three hundred streets and plazas of Seville. Switched on from late November, the display marks Spain's festive season that finishes on 5 January when the Three Kings traditionally bring presents to children. During this period, spectacular shows involving kaleidoscopic lasers and water jets illuminate the Guadalquivir River. In Plaza de San Francisco, projection mapping splashes festive stories on the walls of the Ayuntamiento (City Hall), where the old stone comes alive with images of camels, the Holy Family and the like. Large crowds, including a sea of awestruck young faces, gather to see the visual shows, which are played every 30 to 60 minutes. The plaza is also filled with incredible *belenes* (see page 117) as well as food, drink and craft stalls.

 Free

...Christian devotion peppers the streets, with twist on tradition and local flare.

Nativity scenes across the streets

Throughout December, Seville's hundreds of churches and convents set up elaborate nativity scenes, called *belenes*, to ring in the holiday season. One of the largest is at the Fundación Cajasol in the Plaza de San Francisco, along with an outdoor display beneath the City Hall portico just across the square. Families walk into town together to find their favourites, and end the tour with churros and hot chocolate at spots like *Doña Carmen* (Calle San Eloy 19). An outdoor Christmas market is also set up beside the Catedral, with stands selling every figurine imaginable – flamenco dancers, miniature fruit baskets, elephants. Look for a particularly unique character known as the *caganer:* a young man squatting to defecate. Theories surrounding its origin are inconclusive, but the *caganer* is especially popular in nativity scenes in Catalonia, Valencia and the Balearics.

€ Free

A wealth of treasures, hidden within treasure, preserved not horded, a fusion.

Palacio de la Condesa de Lebrija

Grand yet homely, crammed with curiosities and classical antiquities, Palacio de la Condesa de Lebrija is sure to warm an art-lover's soul on winter days. Built in the sixteenth century, the palace came into its opulent own in the early twentieth century, when keen archaeologist and art collector Doña Regla Manjón Mergelina, Countess of Lebrija, transformed it into an extraordinary space that served as a private residence and a museum to house her collections. The ground floor and courtyard – a glorious fusion of Mudéjar and Renaissance styles – showcases some of the palace's 580 square metres of Roman mosaics, along with Roman, Etruscan and Persian ceramics and sculptures. However, it is the upper floor (accessed on guided tours) that flaunts the countess' eclectic passions to fabulous effect. Here, her private quarters, which include a library, dining room and chapel, gleam with a trove of treasures, from Asian and Moorish art to exquisite French furniture and artefacts unearthed during her excavations.

- https://palaciodelebrija.com
- Charge

*Become well-versed in cosy nooks,
coffee and quatrains, between knowing books...*

Books and brews in La Gata en Bicicleta

When temperatures dip outside, hunker down in this inviting bookshop, café and art gallery hybrid in the *casco antiguo* (Calle Pérez Galdós 22) for a cosy afternoon. Browse the latest titles on interiors, design and poetry; peruse your purchases over a cup of coffee and slice of freshly baked cake; and check out the wall-hung art by local artists showcased as part of rotatory exhibitions. With bare brick walls and wooden tables, it's an inviting space for breakfasts, light lunches of sandwiches and salads, and afternoon teas. If you feel like getting creative, there's a pottery studio on site for classes where you can pick up the basics and take your newly created ceramics home with you. After dark, the chilled hangout serves up local beers and tapas and occasionally hosts music performances and comedy events. A real neighbourhood bar vibe.

- https://www.instagram.com/lagataenbicicletacafe
- Free; charge for events

...learning movement with the rap of clam-like percussion, cutting through, precision and zeal.

Flamenco fever

Seville is one of the birthplaces of flamenco in Andalucía and, at night, soulful beats reverberate through the city streets. Though the art form has roots in Triana, across the Guadalquivir, Santa Cruz is home to an important cultural institution: the Museo del Baile Flamenco. The museum, founded by flamenco star Cristina Hoyos, is housed in a beautiful eighteenth-century building on the foundations of an ancient Roman temple. It was the first – and is still the only – centre of its kind in the world. The modern, innovative space tells the story of the phenomenon through interactive exhibits: hear the rhythms, feel the vibrations – the swish of the full skirts, the clack of the shoes on the wooden floors, the strum of the guitar and the clap of the castanets. Learn about the different styles of flamenco, the fashions and some of the most famous dancers throughout history, from Carmen Amaya and Antonio Gades to Sara Baras and El Güito. The museum is also one of the top places to catch a performance, right in the central atrium.

- https://museodelbaileflamenco.com
- € Charge

The four-cornered badge of identity, resides crafted, glazed and bright; ubiquitous...

Artistic legacy at Centro Cerámica

One thing that's striking about Seville is the abundance of colourful tiles – decorating park benches and fountains, adorning the walls of tapas bars, plastered on the entryways of hotels and churches. These intricate ceramics are so ingrained in the history and architecture of the city that they've become almost a Seville emblem. The Centro Cerámica Triana is a little-known but important museum, providing a unique insight into the artistic heritage and production process. It's housed in the old Fábrica de Cerámica Santa Ana Rodríguez Díaz, one of almost forty working ceramics factories in the neighbourhood during the 1920s. Displays include original kilns, some dating back as far as the sixteenth century, moulds, old craft workshops and potters' wheels. Audiovisual panels and informative tiles provide context and interest for visitors.

https://icas.sevilla.org/espacios/centro-ceramica/informacion-general

€ Charge

*...they are the art in walls but inside,
they hang, clothing with mastered riches.*

Cultural riches in Museo de Bellas Artes

Set in a beautiful former convent, the Museo de Bellas Artes is a knockout from the get-go with its grand entrance and frescoed domed ceilings. One of Spain's most impressive fine-art galleries, the museum's focus is on the city's seventeenth-century Golden Age, with a scattering of works by Spanish and Sevillano artists throughout the fifteenth and twentieth century. There's art from Seville's important Baroque painters like Herrera del Viejo and Juan de Roelas, but the big-hitter is Zurbarán's *Apotheosis of St Thomas Aquinas*. Don't miss the works by Murillo in the apse, crowned by the great *Immaculate Conception* – known as "*La Colosal*" to distinguish it from the other work here with the same name. Below is the same artist's *Virgin and Child*; popularly known as *La Servilleta* because it was said to have been painted on a dinner napkin. Elsewhere, other important pieces include El Greco's portrait of his only son, *Retrato de Jorge Manuel Theotocópuli*.

🖱 https://www.museosdeandalucia.es
€ Charge

That sun-like orb, fortified, squeezed, sweet and heady...

A boutique retreat to warm the heart

Escape the winter chill of colder climes with a stay at one of Seville's hottest addresses. *Las Casas de La Judería*, a labyrinth of traditional houses and palm-shaded courtyards connected by underground tunnels and cobbled paths, feels more like an atmospheric barrio than a hotel. Spend pleasant days wandering the old Jewish quarter of Santa Cruz in gentle temperatures of 16°C to 20°C, free from the sizzling white heat and tourist hordes of summer. Soak up the last lingering rays of sun at the rooftop pool or retreat to the Roman-themed spa for soul-warming massage treatments. And when the cooler evenings draw in, hunker down in the elegant piano room or your guestroom, carefully designed boltholes adorned with fine art, original ceiling beams and striped fabrics.

www.lascasasdelajuderiasevilla.com
€ Charge

...chastened delights fashioned from devotion, sugary joy for all creeds.

Convent sweets fit for a nun

Yemas de San Leandro are not so much forbidden fruit as the sweetest of treats whipped up by Augustinian nuns. Following a 400-year-old recipe – a closely guarded secret – the cloistered nuns create these cone-shaped cakes from sugar, lemon and egg to sell to locals and tourists to support themselves. You can only buy the baked goodies via a revolving tray set within an old wooden door in the Convento de San Leandro, a thirteenth-century institution at Plaza San Ildefonso 1. Put your faith in the process and wait patiently for your treasured box or paper bag holding these individually wrapped delights, which are particularly popular at Christmas. Finding the convent is part of the charm, tucked away in the maze of narrow alleyways. There are other convents with different styles of sweets – the culinary legacy of the Jewish and Muslim populations living in Seville over the centuries.

www.conventosdesevilla.com
€ Charge

Creative endeavour led by skilful guides, years of technique handed down...

Make your own gifts in creative classes

Camila Puya de Arcos grew up aspiring to be a silk painter like her mother: now she leads the Margaret de Arcos artisan label famed for its exquisite scarves, kimonos and fans splashed with vivid floral and Arabic tile designs. The label's new shop, which opened in central Calle Álvarez Quintero in 2025, will also offer silk-painting workshops. Participants will learn about sericulture and the boom in trade during Seville's sixteenth-century Golden Age, before painting a piece of silk traced with a pre-drawn pattern. More into ceramics? Head to Triana, the riverside *azulejo* district whose crafts heritage also goes back centuries. At the Espacio BarroAzul pottery studio, paint a traditional tile using *cuerda seca*, a Mudéjar-era technique designed to keep glazes separate. You'll learn the skill under the watchful gaze of ceramicist Paula and art historian Antonio, an experienced and entertaining duo who guide the sessions.

https://www.barroazul.es
€ Charge

...but taste is personal, so craft your own, synaesthetic science to sample rapture.

Cook up a storm

Seville ranks among Europe's great culinary cities, celebrated for its vibrant tapas culture. For a deeper dive into local gastronomy, Let's Eat the World can arrange a market visit and cooking class tailored to suit small groups, according to tastes and location. The hosts – owner Yetunde Oshodi-Fraudeau and chef Sam – show participants how to create classics like *salmorejo* (chilled creamy tomato soup), *arròs negro* (squid-ink rice), and *torrijas* (Spanish-style French toast). At Hispalia, explore culinary techniques from Roman Baetica (southern Spain), including how *famed garum* – fermented fish sauce, a staple of the ancient Mediterranean diet – was made, and how to cook with it. The owners, a scientist and a sommelier, produce their own wine, beer, cheese and garum itself using revived ancestral methods. Their space, appropriately, is next to the underground archaeological museum, Antiquarium de Sevilla, at Las Setas market – sample their wares at the *Hispalia* bar.

> https://letseattheworld.com
> € Charge

A paradise crackles and climbs to the heavens, ritualised in a soft glow.

Bonfires and blessings at Candlemas

Candlemas, on 2 February, marks the presentation of Jesus at the temple and the ceremonial purification of Mary, an age-old ritual still profound across Andalucía. While Seville is famed for the grand pageantry of Semana Santa, Candlemas (La Candelaria) reveals a gentler side of devotion. In parish churches across the city, soft candlelight dances on *azulejos* as worshippers gather for blessings and intimate *besamanos* (ceremonial greetings) before the Virgen de la Candelaria. Incense wafts through the night air, mingling with murmured prayers. Beyond the centre, barrios like Polígono Sur and La Oliva host modest *procesiones*: statues carried out after evening Mass, candles flickering against winter skies. Further afield, villages in the Sierra Sur come alive with hundreds of glowing bonfires, music and communal warmth. Though quieter than Easter, Candlemas offers a soulful, crowd-free snapshot into Andalusian faith, entwined in neighbourhood pride and the soft glow of shared devotion.

€ Free

Contributors

Dayna Camilleri Clarke is an award-winning British travel writer who has lived in Malta for the past decade, after more than seventeen years working and travelling around the Southern Mediterranean. She studied in Spain and has returned many times, with Seville a city she always finds herself drawn back to. Her work has appeared in *BBC Travel*, *Wanderlust* and *Time Out*, and she spent several years as editor of Air Malta's in-flight magazine. She also has a weakness for trying local delicacies – research, she insists, not indulgence.

Andrew and Suzanne Edwards are the authors of *Andalucia: A Literary Guide for Travellers*, a tour in the footsteps of writers inspired by the region. In addition to three other books of literary travel, they have also written *Down to the Sunless Sea*, a biography of Samuel Taylor Coleridge's time in the Mediterranean including the south of the Iberian Peninsula. They have updated Bradt's *Emilia Romagna* and are presently working on *The Culture Lover's Guide to Seville* to be published in 2027. Andrew is also a Spanish and Italian translator.

John Elmes is a London-based writer, journalist and editor. He fell in love with Andalucía the first time he visited, way back when on a school trip in the early 2000s. John has returned to Spain – including Seville – many times since, and his love for its culture and gastronomy deepens with every visit.

After two decades at the *Evening Standard*, **Jo Fernández** became a freelance travel writer, travelling the world for a variety of newspapers, magazines and digital platforms. She particularly loves Latin America, the Caribbean and Spain, and has just published *The Tapas Lover's Guide to Madrid*.

Travel writer **Esme Fox** has written and updated several guidebooks to Spain as well as countless articles. She has lived in Barcelona for the past ten years, but was previously based in Andalucía and still travels regularly to Seville – one of her favourite cities. She finds something new to love about the place each time she visits and enjoys getting lost among its romantic alleyways.

Megan Lloyd is a Texas-born, Seville-based travel writer who has updated guidebooks to Spain and written numerous stories on its cuisine and culture. She has lived in Seville since 2017 but first stepped foot in the city in 2011. Since then she's become an expert in Sevillano culture: she regularly eats dinner at 10pm, can dance *sevillana*, and loves nothing more than a drink and tapa on a sunny patio.

London-based writer and editor **Polly Mackintosh** lived and worked in Seville for many joyous months, during which she enjoyed more than her fair share of icy *cañas* and tapas in the sun, and now visits as often as she can.

Joanne Owen is a Pembrokeshire-born, London-based writer, editor and book reviewer, and the author of several acclaimed novels and works of non-fiction for children and young adults. Joanne has a long-time love of history-steeped European cities, with Seville capturing her heart as a result of its infectiously joyous spirit.

Joanna Reeves is a travel writer and editor who has worked on a plethora of Rough Guides, including co-authoring and editing the first-ever edition of the *Pocket Rough Guide to Seville*. She fell in love with the city from the first time she visited, from its food and culture to its vibrant street scene, and has widely travelled the wider Andalucía region in search of the prettiest White Towns – Ronda is up there at the top.

Adam Turner is an award-winning freelance travel writer hailing from Northeast England. A lifelong Hispanophile, he spent several years living in Seville and Barcelona in his late twenties. Today, he is a destination expert on Andalucía, with work spanning Granada's tapas scene, the Sherry Triangle and insider guides to Seville. He's written for publications including *Condé Nast Traveller, The Mail on Sunday*, *Time Out*, *The Independent,* and *The Guardian*. Follow him on Instagram @adtwriter.

Travel writer **Fiona Flores Watson** has been based in Seville for more than twenty years, and is still endlessly inspired by the city – especially the intersection between its long history and modern-day icons, as well as its sublime tapas scene. She writes for *The Telegraph* and *Times*, among others, and also works as a tour guide and translator in Seville.

Credits

City Stories: Seville Seasons
Concept: Beth Williams
Editor: Joanna Reeves
Proofreader and indexer: Penny Phenix
Picture Editor: Piotr Kala
Picture Manager: Tom Smyth
Production Operations Manager: Katie Bennett
Publishing Technology Manager: Rebeka Davies
Head of Publishing: Sarah Clark
Photo credits: Parisa/Flickr under CC BY-NC-SA 2.0 license 106; amadoviews/Noches de La Maestranza 98; Feria del Libro de Sevilla 89; Gabriel Navas/Barro Azul 132; Italica Festival 63; La Terraza Doña Maria 38; Niccolo Guasti/Icónica Santalucía 41; Public domain 131; Shutterstock 4, 7, 8, 11, 12, 15, 16, 19, 20, 23, 24, 27, 28, 31, 32, 34, 37, 42, 45, 46, 49, 50, 53, 54, 57, 58, 60, 64, 67, 68, 71, 72, 75, 76, 79, 80, 83, 84, 86, 90, 93, 94, 97, 101, 102, 105, 109, 110, 112, 115, 116, 119, 120, 123, 124, 127, 135, 136; Vanessa Clarke 128

Printed by Finidr in Czech Republic

A catalogue record for this book is available from the British Library.

All Rights Reserved
© 2026 Apa Digital AG
License edition © Apa Publications Ltd UK

First Edition 2026

ISBN: 9781835295069

No part of this book may be reproduced, stored in a retrieval system or transmitted in any form or means electronic, mechanical, photocopying, recording or otherwise, without prior written permission from Apa Publications.

No part of this book may be used or reproduced in any manner for the purpose of training artificial intelligence technologies or systems.

Every effort has been made to ensure that this publication is accurate, free from safety risks, and provides accurate information. However, changes and errors are inevitable. The publisher is not responsible for any resulting loss, inconvenience, injury or safety concerns arising from the use of this book.

Distribution
UK, Ireland and Europe
Apa Publications (UK) Ltd;
mail@roughguides.com
United States and Canada
Two Rivers;
ips@ ingramcontent.com

Australia and New Zealand
Woodslane;
info@woodslane.com.au
Worldwide
Apa Publications (UK) Ltd;
mail@roughguides.com

Special Sales, Content Licensing and CoPublishing
Rough Guides can be purchased in bulk quantities at discounted prices. We can create special editions, personalized jackets and corporate imprints tailored to your needs.
mail@roughguides.com
http://roughguides.com

EU Representative
LOGOS EUROPE,
9 rue Nicolas Poussin, 17000,
LA ROCHELLE, France
Contact@logoseurope.eu;
+33 (0) 667937378

Index

A
AIRE Ancient Baths 10
Alcázar gardens 65
Alcornocales natural park 29
Alfalfa 104
Antigua Fábrica de Tabacos 51
Arabic bathhouse 70
Aracena 100
Arco de la Macarena 74
art. See also museums and galleries
art and craft workshops
 pottery decorating classes 133
 silk-painting classes 133

B
bars 73
 Bar Garlochí 107
 Cervecería Geralda 70
 rooftop bars 39
 Taberna Álvaro Peregil 29
bathhouse 70
belenes 114

bike-sharing scheme 103
bike tours 103
birdlife and birdwatching 14, 15
bookshops 121

C
cafés 121
CaixaForum 85
Carmen, the opera 51
Carmona 111
Casa de Pilatos 48
cave tour. *See* Gruta de las Maravillas

Centro Cerámica 125
Cervantes 33
Concertada Dehesa de Abajo 14
Convento de San Leandro 130
cooking classes 130
Córdoba 30
Cortes de la Frontera nature reserve 29
Coto de Doñana National Park 14
Cueva de la Pileta 52
cycling 103

D
dance. See flamenco
Dehesa de Abajo, Reserva Natural Concertada 14

E
El Rocío pilgrimage 22

F
festivals and events 5
    Candlemas 137
    Christmas 6, 114, 117
    El Orgullo 36
    El Rocío pilgrimage 22
    European Film Festival 91
    Feria de Abril 17
    Feria del Libro Sevilla 88
    Feria de Santa Ana 82
    Festival de Cine Europeo 91
    Fiesta de los Patios (Córdoba) 30
    Holy Week 13
    Icónica Santalucía Sevilla Fest 40
    Interestelar Sevilla music festival 21
    International Dance Festival of Itálica 62
    Noche en Blanco 95
    Noches de La Maestranza 6, 99
    Noches en los Jardines del Real Alcázar 65
    Pride festival 36
    Recoveco Market 25
    Romería El Rocío 22
    Semana Santa 13
    Spring Fair 17
    Virgen del Carmen procession 59
flamenco 47, 66, 122
food and drink 44, 108. See also markets, restaurants
    beer 73
    caracoles (snails) 6, 44
    cooking classes 134
    fish 81
    gelato (ice cream) 18, 77
    market visits, guided 134
    olive oil 108
    tapas 70
    vino de naranja 92
    wine 92
    Yemas de San Leandro 130
football 78

G
Galería de los Grutesco 65
Galería Taberna Ánima 47
Game of Thrones location 62, 65
gardens 65. See also national parks and nature reserves
    Alcázar gardens 65
    Jardines de Murillo 88
Gruta de las Maravillas 100
Guadalquivir River 6, 55, 59, 69

H
Hospital de la Caridad 43

I
International Dance Festival of Itálica 62
Interestelar Sevilla music festival 21
Itálica 62

J
Jardines de Murillo 88
Jueves Market 56

K
kayaking 69

L
La Fuga Librerías 96
La Muralla Almohade 74
Las Casas de La Judería 129
Las Salinas 43
Leal, Murillo and Valdés 26
literary tour 33

M

Margaret de Arcos designer label 133
markets 56
    Jueves Market 56
    Mercadillo del Juevas 56
    Mercado de Feria 56
    Recoveco Market 25
Mercadillo del Juevas 56
Mercado de Feria 56
miracle of Nuestra Señora del Rocío 22
Mudéjar bathhouse 10
Muralla Almohade, La 74
museums and galleries 26
    Alfalfa area galleries 104
    CaixaForum 85
    Centro Cerámica 125
    commercial galleries 104
    Espacio Derivado 26
    Espacío Sacáis 26
    free admission nights 95
    Galería Haurie 26
    Galería Rafael Ortiz 26
    Museo de Bellas Artes 126
    Museo del Balle Flamenco 122
    Noche en Blanco events 95
    Palacio de la Condesa de Librija 118
music. *See also* dance, festivals and events
    flamenco 47
    opera 40
    rooftop music venues 39

N

national parks and nature reserves. *See also* gardens
    Cortes de la Frontera nature reserve 29
    Reserva Natural Concertada Dehesa de Abajo 14
    Parque Nacional Coto de Doñana 14
    Parque Natural de la Sierra de Grazalema 29
    Parque Natural de los Alcornocales 29

O

orange blossom 18

P

Palacio de la Condesa de Librija 118
Palacio de Las Duñas 43
Plaza de España 40
Plaza de Toros de la Real Maestranza 99
prehistoric cave paintings 52
Pueblos Blancos 29

R

Ramón Sánchez-Pizjuán Stadium 78
Recoveco Market 25
restaurants 81. *See also* food and drink
Roman theatre 62
Ronda 29
rooftop bars 39

S

Santa Cruz 26, 48
seasons 6
    Spring 9, 18
    Summer 37, 61
    Autumn 87
    Winter 113
shopping 18
    art 104
    azahar oil 18
    La Fuga Librerías 96
    Recoveco Market 25
Sierra de Grazalema Natural Park 29
soccer 89
spa 10
stand-up paddleboarding 69

T

Triana 82

U

UNESCO listing 30

V

views 39
Virgen del Carmen procession 59

W

wellness facilities 10
White Towns 29
wildlife 14. See also birdlife and birdwatching
wine. *See* food and drink